ᒥᖅᓱᕈᓐᓇᖅᑐᖓ
MIQSURUNNAQTUNGA
I CAN SEW

ᐅᓇ ᒥᖅᑯᑎ.

Una miqquti.

This is a needle.

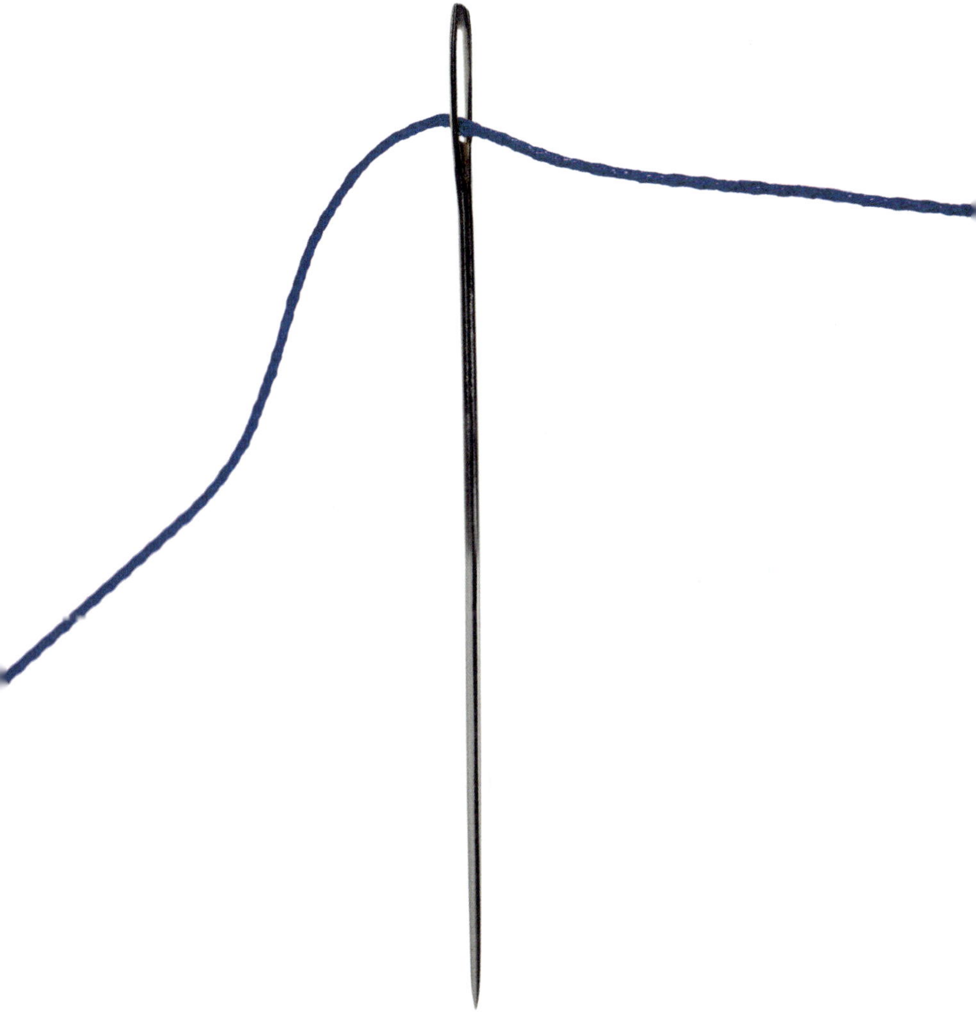

ᐅᓇ ᐃᕙᓗᒃᓴᐅᑎ.

Una ivaluksauti.

This is thread.

ᐅᓇ ᑎᑭᖅ.

Una tikiq.

This is a thimble.

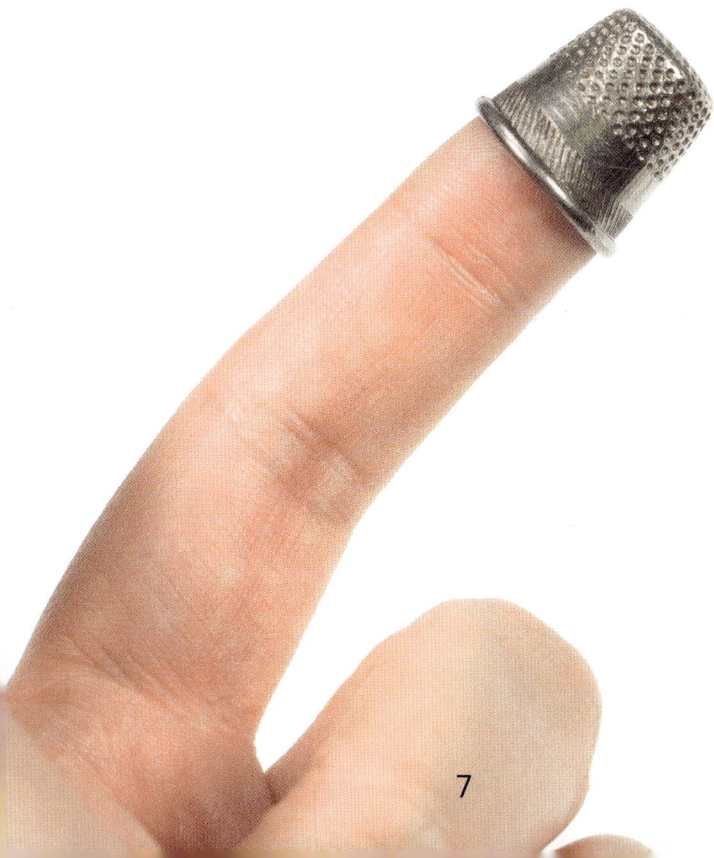

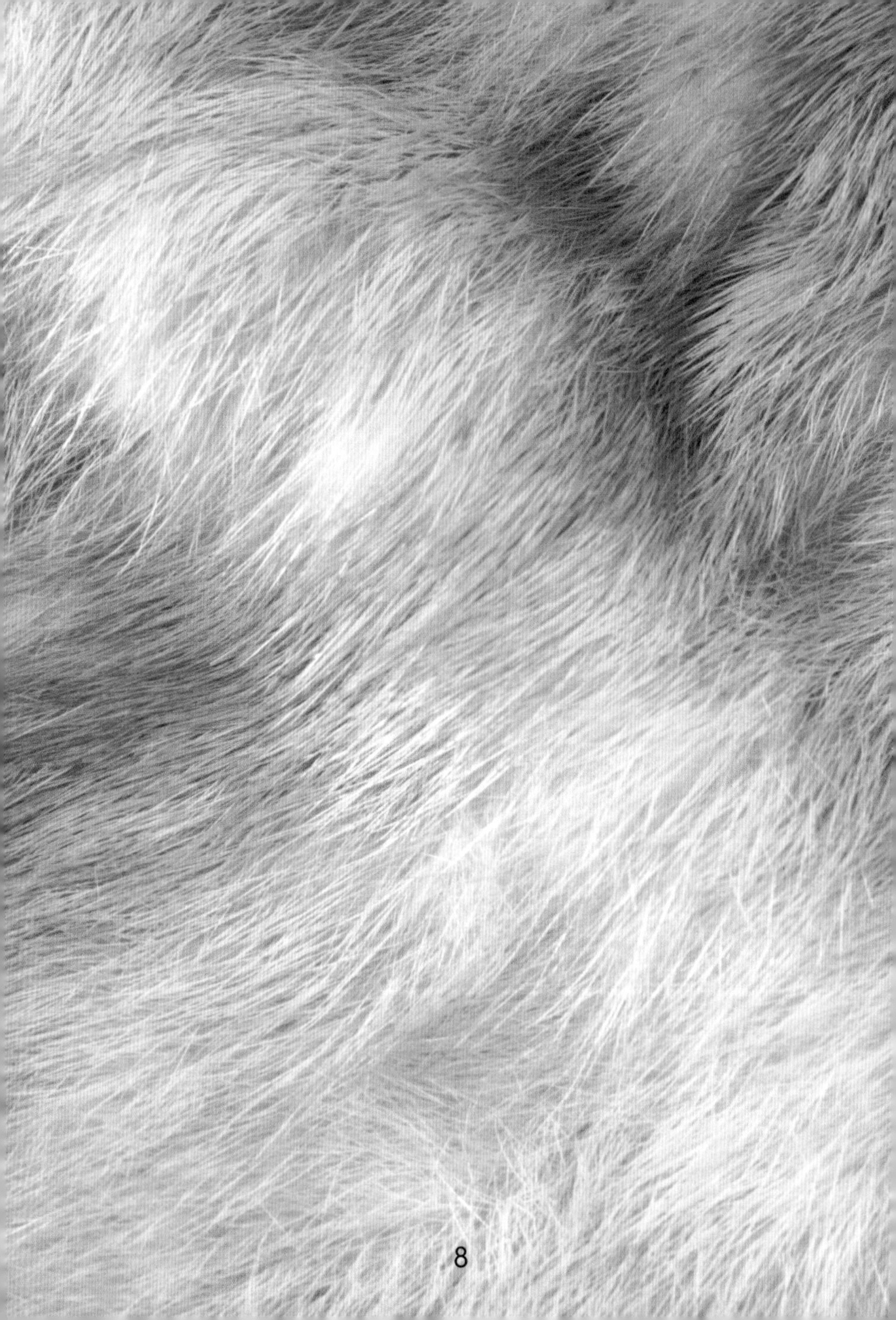

ᐅᓇ ᓄᐃᓚᒃᓴᖅ.

Una nuilaksaq.

This is fur.

ᐅᓇ ᑲᐱᑕᒃᓴᖅ.

Una kapitaksaq.

This is fabric.

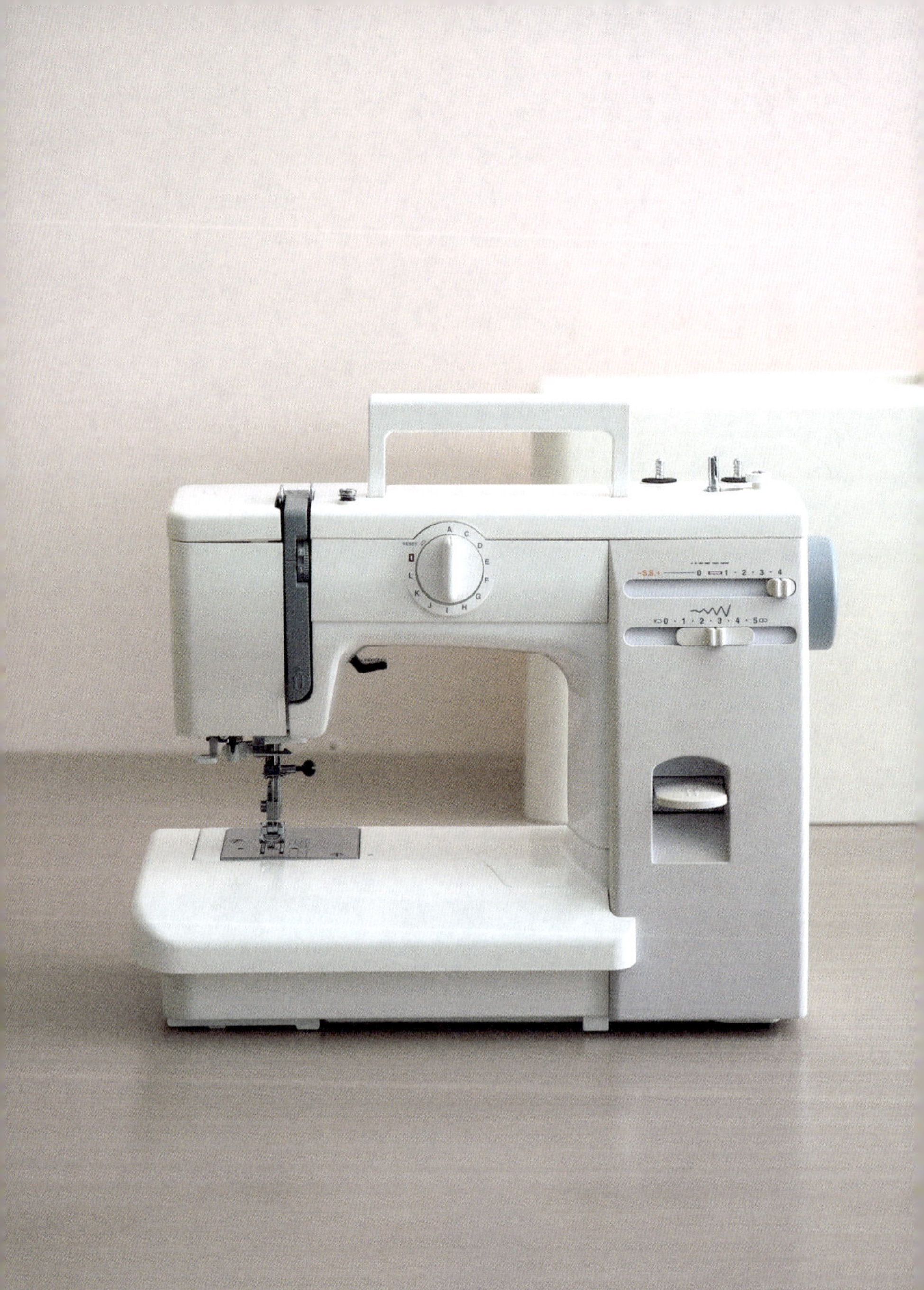

ᐅᓇ ᒥᖅᓲᑎ.

Una miqsuuti.

This is a sewing machine.

ᐅᓇ ᖁᓕᑦᑕᐅᔭᖅ.

Una qulittaujaq.

This is a parka.

Nunavummi